# dePictions

Editorial Cartoons by Michael de Adder

Nimbus Publishing Limited
3731 Mackintosh St, Halifax, NS B3K 5A5
(902) 455-4286 nimbus.ca

Printed and bound in Canada

Author photo: Nicole Lapierre Photography
Interior design: Jenn Embree
Cover design: Michael de Adder
NB#: 1095

Library and Archives Canada Cataloguing in Publication

De Adder, Michael, 1967-, artist
dePictions : editorial cartoons / by Michael de Adder.
Issued in print and electronic formats.
ISBN 978-1-77108-089-7 (pbk.).--ISBN 978-1-77108-090-3 (pdf)

1. Editorial cartoons—Canada. 2. Canadian wit and humor, Pictorial (English). 3. Comic books, strips, etc. I. Title.

NC1449.D42A4 2013 741.5'971 C2013-903460-9
C2013-903461-7

Canada Council for the Arts Conseil des arts du Canada

NOVA SCOTIA
Communities, Culture and Heritage

Nimbus Publishing acknowledges the financial support for its publishing activities from the Government of Canada through the Canada Book Fund (CBF) and the Canada Council for the Arts, and from the Province of Nova Scotia through the Department of Communities, Culture and Heritage.

FOR MEAGHAN

# Contents

# Foreword

Michael de Adder, one of the most widely read cartoonists in Canada, was born and raised in Moncton, New Brunswick, but his cartooning roots are in Halifax. His early foray into the subversive profession began in the '90s at Halifax's alternative weekly the *Coast,* with his much-loved inaugural strip "Walterworld" (dedicated to the skewering of then-Halifax mayor Walter Fitzgerald). From there to his first years freelancing for the *Halifax Chronicle-Herald*, to his term as full-time editorial cartoonist for the *Daily News*, to his animated editorial cartoons for the regional CBC broadcaster and beyond, Mike's cartoons have covered every inch of Halifax and the province of Nova Scotia. Beyond that, from his regular positions at the *Ottawa Hill Times*, the *Toronto Star*, and other major dailies, to syndication throughout Canada and internationally, his cartoons have brought him fans and notoriety from around the globe.

So what makes Mike's cartoons so popular? A whole pile of things, but first and foremost, as *Herald* columnist Jim Meek so aptly put it during Mike's early days at the Herald, "He has a tremendous sense of fun." Mike's cartoons have the ability to make a reader giddy even while making a point that tears his target apart. His drawing talent, caricature skills, and creativity all contribute to this special gift. And in a profession that depends on getting there first, Mike's ability to react quickly to breaking news stories is second to none.

That's the professional formula that makes de Adder such a successful cartoonist. But who is he, really? Editorial cartoonists are seen by many as the court jesters of journalism, so people often presume we are hilariously entertaining in person. In truth, many of us are odd characters… eccentric introverts or cynical critics emotionally deformed by years spent holed up in solitary confinement, scrawling out visual spitballs to fire at public figures. de Adder, on the other hand, walks the walk and talks the talk. He is personable, zany, and funny as hell, with just enough mischief mixed in to make it interesting.

At the closing banquet of a Canadian cartoonists' convention in Halifax a few years back, Mike was seated beside federal Conservative cabinet minister Peter MacKay, who had been invited into the lion's den to give the keynote speech. I observed from across the table as de Adder and MacKay swapped stories of their rugby-playing glory days of youth. On several occasions while MacKay was talking, Mike would put his arm around MacKay and look across the table in our direction with a classic "photo-op" smile. MacKay would instantly respond by turning in the same direction with his well-practiced photo-op smile, only to discover there was, in fact, no one taking pictures.

Such is the humour of Mike de Adder. Giddy, infectious, and cutting. In another life, he could have been a stand-up comic. His readers, however, are just thrilled he does what does.

***Bruce MacKinnon***

editorial cartoonist for the *Halifax Chronicle-Herald*

# A Brief History of Time

On the morning of February 11, 2008, just as *Halifax Daily News* staff were beginning their day, management started to frantically gather the four departments—editorial, production, circulation, and advertising—for a meeting that would take place immediately in the newsroom overlooking Halifax Harbour. The meeting would include everybody, and Transcontinental management seemed abnormally impatient to get it started.

The people they were gathering were not just employees at a newspaper, they were family. There were lifelong friends, married couples, common-law couples, and exes, all working side-by-side. At company barbecues, kids with two parents who worked for the newspaper were playing with kids with two other parents who worked for the newspaper. If the publisher had good news to deliver, it was doubly good for these families. But the reverse was also true.

Everybody could tell the news out of this meeting was going to be doubly bad.

There is an unwritten rule in the newspaper business that if a reporter is on the phone conducting an interview

*One of the last cartoons to appear in the* Halifax Daily News. *Stephane Dion being bullied by Stephen Harper and Jim Flaherty.*

that everybody within earshot either stays quiet or respectfully leaves the space so the interviewer can do their job. Interviews are a key ingredient in news gathering, and it is in everybody's interest for an interview to go off professionally.

The manager who was herding the section around me started to goad a reporter in the middle of one of these early morning interviews.

It seemed highly unusual that a manager at a newspaper would do such a thing. The reporter put her hand over the mouthpiece, told the manager quite directly that she was in the middle of an interview and to please be quiet. In a no-nonsense manner the manager told her to hang up the phone, and that everybody had to attend this meeting.

In that moment, my heart sank. I knew what the meeting was about. I said to the manager, "The *Daily News* is folding, isn't it?"

## THE BEGINNING

I became a cartoonist completely by chance.

I was in the right place at the wrong time. I was sitting in the lounge of the Fine Arts Building at Mount Allison University with several other students, minding my own business, when Derrick Sleep walked in. I was in my second year studying fine arts, on my way to a degree in painting.

Sleep was a fine arts student, but he was also the cartoon editor at the *Argosy*, the university's independent student newspaper. It was the beginning of the semester, so he was asking every student with a pulse if they'd be interested in drawing cartoons for the paper. It didn't seem to matter whether they could draw or not.

The *Argosy* had a two-page cartoon section. The cartoons were drawn by students. Some were so bad they were funny, and others were so bad, well, they were just bad. When reading the "Comix" page, rarely did a reader laugh at the intended joke. But by national standards, the *Argosy* was a very well-read university newspaper. It garnered a lot of local reaction and a lot of letters to the editor.

When Sleep asked me if I was interested, to this day I don't remember saying yes, but I don't remember saying no either. Not saying no seemed to be enough for Sleep, and like that, I was a cartoonist. My foray into the cartoon world began with a childish comic strip called "Otterman." "Otterman" was sophomoric, silly, and at times, crude. It garnered mail and made a lot of people mad.

Even though it showed little promise of what would come later, "Otterman" taught me the basics—how to tell a story using panels, how to be funny using timing, and how to stay on deadline, ironically something that was lacking in actual painting classes.

As I went into my third year I became more political. It was 1988, and it was a time of budget cuts and internal strife

*The Unfriendly Giant. A cartoon from the* Argosy, *Mount Allison's school newspaper.*

at Mount Allison. The conditions were perfect for somebody drawing cartoons about campus politics. I started a weekly single-panel cartoon on the president of the university. The president at that time was quite unpopular, and my cartoons certainly didn't help him out.

Cartooning became as important to me as my fine arts classes. I remember my printmaking professor one day praising me for my work. But it wasn't for the prints I did in his class, it was for the cartoons about the university president in the *Argosy*.

While I was cutting my teeth on campus politics, a major event was taking place on the federal stage, an election campaign between Brian Mulroney and John Turner. This was no ordinary election. It was a referendum on where the country would go for the next one hundred years. It all had to do with something called the North American Free Trade Agreement (NAFTA). Mulroney wanted it and Turner opposed it. A vote for Mulroney was a vote for NAFTA. A vote for Turner was a vote for the status quo. Canada was in turmoil. Universities were at the boiling point.

Two things happened that would cement my future as an editorial cartoonist. The first was I drew the cartoon at right.

The *Argosy* came out on Thursday, and by Friday morning most people saw this cartoon. By Friday afternoon it was being posted across campus. I'd go by a bulletin board and there it was. I'd go to class and it was posted in the hall. I'd go to a party in one of the dorms and it was taped on doors. It was all over the place.

During my time at Mount A, I had a gallery showing of my paintings on campus. Maybe a couple of hundred people saw the show, and the turnout was considered very high. People who attend galleries are usually people interested in gallery work—educated artsy types or people pretending to be educated artsy types. But everybody reads cartoons. Professors, students, plumbers, teachers...everybody. And it was clear everybody read this cartoon.

Suddenly I wanted to affect people like this all the time.

Up until this point I barely knew the work of any real

political cartoonists. There was no internet in the '80s, and I didn't grow up with an influential cartoonist in the city newspaper, like Bruce MacKinnon did reading Bob Chambers. I pretty much grew up with *MAD magazine* and whatever freelance cartoon appeared in the *Moncton Times & Transcript*.

I needed to do some research, so I went to the Ralph Pickard Bell Library and there the second thing that would cement my future as a cartoonist happened. I was thumbing through the section that contained books by editorial cartoonists and saw three books by a cartoonist named Aislin. I opened the pages and could hardly contain my enthusiasm. This was the bridge between art and cartooning I'd been looking for. I was hooked.

## AFTER UNIVERSITY

When you attend university everything is handed to you—food on your meal plan, room and board, heat, and hot water. It's like you're still living at home. The difference is you don't have a mother to wash that big pile of clothes on your floor every so often.

Even when you move off-campus, you still have this magical money, which the banking world refers to as a loan, sitting in an account waiting to be spent on beer. Life is on hold until that moment you are thrust into that cold, harsh emptiness called real life.

Cartooning came relatively easy to me in university. And no wonder, since the job of cartoon editor was wanted only by me. I was my own editor, which meant I ran all my own stuff, no matter how bad or offensive. I didn't need to make money so long as the magical bank account didn't run out.

But because I didn't have to fight to be published, I wasn't nearly as good a cartoonist as I thought I was. The work I was drawing was more appropriate for alternative magazines, not mainstream newspapers.

To my surprise, editorial cartoon jobs weren't being thrown off turnip trucks to whoever wanted one. They were at a premium. At that time, Canada had a population of about thirty million, and there were under thirty working cartoonists in the whole country. One in a million Canadians was a cartoonist. It was harder to be a professional cartoonist than to be a professional painter.

Oblivious to the realities of the profession, I thought I'd walk into the offices of the *Moncton Times & Transcript*, they'd hand me my key, and balloons and confetti would drop from the ceiling when I walked in the next morning with my pens and paper.

What actually happened was the editorial page editor took one look at my portfolio and said, "I have no budget for an extra reporter, let alone an editorial cartoonist." But he did like one cartoon in my portfolio and offered me twelve dollars on condition I take out the word buggers. “The Irvings frown upon sodomy being mentioned in their newspapers,” he explained.

I did what he said and waited a month to get my twelve dollars mailed to me. This was going to be harder than I thought.

## IN THE WILDERNESS

I worked at Hub Meat Packers for a time loading trucks full of beef. I did that for nearly a year before I panicked one day and saw myself as a lifer. I quit and moved to Halifax.

My plan was to be a painter, or if that didn't work, a cartoonist. It was a flip of the coin. My destiny would be decided by what paid my rent. I still had to find a real job, but I had money saved from loading beef, so I could be a little choosy about employment. And, more importantly, I could paint and draw when not looking for work.

I worked hard.

I had four large paintings by the end of the first year and at one point four cartoons I'd sent as a package published in New Brunswick's *Telegraph Journal*. The *Telegraph* paid fifty dollars apiece and said they'd buy more on one condition—that I didn't overload them with piles of work. Well,

*Drawn in 1993, this is one of the first cartoons I drew for the* Telegraph Journal.

within one week I was overloading them with piles of work and they stopped buying.

Truthfully, overloading wasn't my real problem at the *TJ*, because if I was overloading them with work they liked, they would have published it. I was overloading them with stuff they couldn't, or wouldn't, print. I still had too much of an edge for mainstream newspapers. That, and I attacked everything with viciousness.

Frank McKenna was a saint in New Brunswick, at least as far as newspaper reporting was concerned. I attacked

McKenna with the same vehemence that I attacked Brian Mulroney. And I attacked Mulroney like I attacked the plague. Newspapers weren't going to publish my work until I toned down my cartoons.

You don't need an elephant gun if you're hunting squirrels. And sometimes in politics the story is a squirrel. I was shooting an elephant gun at everything that moved.

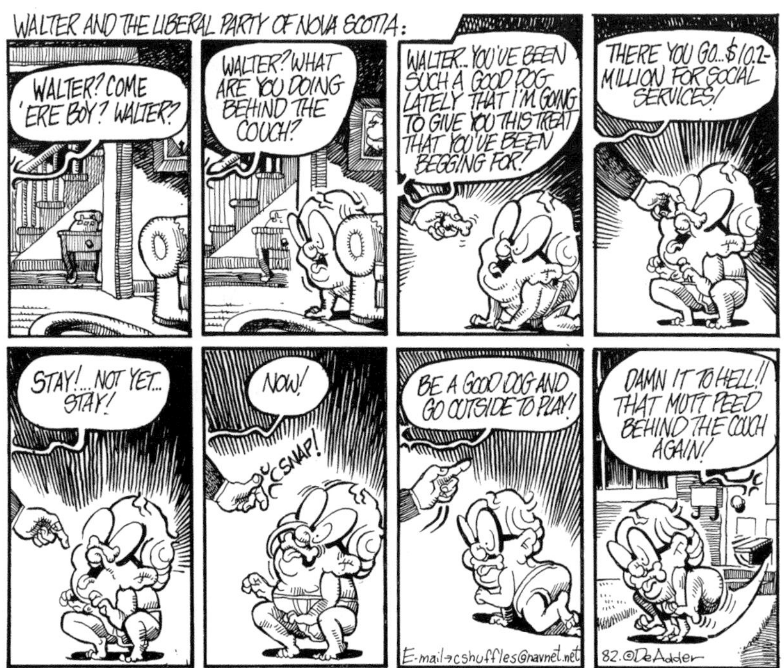


*"Walterworld," which appeared in the* Coast *for five years.*

## FOOT IN THE DOOR

I didn't see any progress on the cartoon front until I started a political cartoon strip called "Walterworld" for the *Coast*, Halifax's alternative weekly. "Walterworld" was about the mayor of Halifax at the time, Walter Fitzgerald. Fitzgerald was colourful, fearless, and prone to making gaffes. He was perfect fodder for a cartoonist.

"Walterworld" could be absurd at times, and very good at other times. I started to make a small name for myself. But I wasn't Michael de Adder: I was that guy who did "Walterworld." The *Coast* paid me twelve dollars a week. I'd have made more sewing sneakers in Bangladesh. But I had a foot in the door and a byline in Halifax.

At the time, I couldn't really call myself a cartoonist. I could call myself a waiter who drew funny pictures as a sideline.

## THE *CHRONICLE-HERALD*

It was around this time that I met Bruce MacKinnon, the award-winning cartoonist for the *Chronicle-Herald*, on the street. I walked around the corner and we almost ran into each other. I stopped him and told him who I was. He kindly offered to show me around his office sometime. I

Cabinet Shuffles by Michael De Adder

*My first strip at the* Chronicle Herald *was a strip called "Cabinet Shuffles."*

can't remember, but I probably dropped by the next day. I was desperate for any advice. There is no handbook to becoming a cartoonist. You mostly go about it blind and in the dark.

MacKinnon gave me advice and introduced me to a few people, Bev Dauphinee being one. I started a weekly strip called "Cabinet Shuffles" for her op-ed page on Wednesdays. Just like that, I was in the *Chronicle-Herald*. It was a small but mighty step.

The key to cartooning is getting a deadline. It forces you to work. And only by working do you get better. There is no point where you can clearly distinguish when you get good, or if you ever get good. It is slow and gradual. Slowly the drawings get better as slowly the ideas improve.

As I improved, the *Chronicle-Herald* gave me more work. And in giving me more work, I kept improving. I got picked up by the *Saint John Times Globe* and the *Hill Times*, to this day my longest continuous cartoon assignment. Suddenly I had enough work and quit my job as a waiter.

## THE *HALIFAX DAILY NEWS*

In the summer of 2000 opportunity came knocking. Theo Moudakis, Halifax's other editorial cartoonist, decided to take a job at the *Toronto Star*. I was offered his job at the *Daily News*. To my complete surprise, I didn't immediately jump at the idea.

A job was always the dream. But by then I owed my entire career to the *Herald*. The *Daily News* was the *Herald*'s direct competitor in Halifax.

There's a big problem working as a freelance cartoonist—you never get a paid vacation. When a freelancer takes a vacation, it costs them in missed income. They can't just leave and go away. They leave after working overtime to get work done in advance, or don't get paid for the work that's not done and then come back behind the eight ball. It's a work spiral all the time.

I had to take the job. There was no choice.

Once, at a cartoonist's conference, Terry "Aislin" Mosher showed me the silver ring on his finger. It was composed of seven or eight skulls. He likes to say the ring represents all the editors he outlasted at the *Montreal Gazette* in a thirty-five-year period. I didn't know it at the time, but in my eight years at the *Daily News*, I would see six different newsroom editors. (I could have had my own skull ring.)

The *Daily News* had some serious ups and downs. But it soldiered on as the little paper that could. For a small newspaper, it could garner big attention—sometimes thanks to me. When Jerry Falwell died I drew the cartoon on the right.

On the day this cartoon appeared a local Halifax pastor pulled all his ads from the newspaper in protest. Because of the pastor's actions, it became a news story in the cartoon world. Cagle Post, a U.S. political cartoon site, wrote a story about it that went viral in the United States. On his site, Daryl Cagle included the contact information for the cartoonist—me.

The email started pouring in three, seven, eleven at a time. I would press "get mail" and there would be three more. A few seconds later I'd press it again and there were four. This went on for two days. Thousands of emails. Literally.

My email crashed. I emptied the folder and it filled back up again. I loved it.

Editors generally liked it when I got in trouble. I could count on one hand how many times my cartoons got axed. But when Joseph Ratzinger was elected Pope Benedict XVI I drew the cartoon on the next page.

*One of the most controversial cartoons at the* Daily News. *Jerry Falwell depicted appearing in hell after his death. May 16, 2007.*

My editor at the time was a Catholic and didn't want to run it. I pushed back. I argued that I was also Catholic and this cartoon illustrated perfectly how moderate Catholics felt. Up until that moment I had never had a problem getting a cartoon into the paper that was good and also made a political point. But in the end I lost and it didn't run.

*A cartoon that was axed by the* Halifax Daily News *and wound up winning the Golden Spike Award.*

A few months later, I went to the Association of American Editorial Cartoonists annual convention where it won the Golden Spike Award for the best cartoon that was killed by an editor.

After that, the editor never axed another cartoon.

## THE *HALIFAX DAILY NEWS* FOLDS

There's a feeling when you work for a newspaper that you are working for something special. News gathering is, after all, an important animal in the whole democratic food chain. So the idea that a newspaper could fold seems ludicrous, even to a personal witness to declining circulation and dwindling ad revenue. As bad as things get, there remains the belief that it'll all work out in the end. It's a newspaper. It's rooted in history.

So, when you stand in a room with all your friends and people you call family, and somebody tells you that the newspaper you work for is closing immediately, it doesn't make sense. It makes as much sense as somebody telling you there's no more air, we used it all up.

The day the *Halifax Daily News* folded, I was lucky. I had been freelancing for Brunswick News Inc. since 2001. NBI offered me a job working for both the *Moncton Times & Transcript* and the *Fredericton Daily Gleaner.* I also did some political animating for CBC that proved to be fun but labour-intensive.

## MY CAREER PATH MAKES A FULL CIRCLE

The *Chronicle-Herald* is rare. It sees the editorial cartoon as an essential piece of the newspaper experience. The paper already has Bruce MacKinnon on staff, one of the best editorial cartoonists in the country. MacKinnon has developed such a following over twenty-five years that subscribers feel ripped off when he takes any time off, leaving the *Herald* with a large hole when he goes on vacation. Sometimes I feel my cartoon is like spackling compound trying to fill this enormous hole.

And while I fill in for Bruce MacKinnon at the *Chronicle-Herald*, it is truly ironic that I also fill in for Theo Moudakis at the *Toronto Star* (after all, it was Moudakis whom I replaced at the *Daily News*. Editorial cartooning is a strange bird.)

Roy Peterson, the *Vancouver Sun*'s former award-winning political cartoonist, said that when you're a cartoonist sometimes you have a bad day, sometimes you have a bad week, and other times you have a bad year.

When a cartoonist has a bad day, everybody knows it. The cartoon isn't funny or doesn't work. It's like being a field goal kicker on the football team. Everybody knows when you miss. But on the other hand, everybody knows when you split the uprights. You're the hero or the bum. And some days you're both.

When *E. coli* broke out in a restaurant in the Miramichi, I drew the cartoon above for the *Moncton Times & Transcript*.

*The cartoon that caused a controversy in Miramichi.*

The restaurant in question was a popular hangout in the Miramichi.

A tweet came in asking me what I had against the Miramichi. I answered it and another came in. Then another. By lunchtime there was a website telling people to boycott the newspaper over their unfair portrayal of the Miramichi. There were endless comments on my Facebook page. I tried to debate people at first, but it was futile. Arguing with people on the Internet is like playing cards with a sock. I just rode it out.

The following day the *Times & Transcript* apologized for the cartoon.

With social media, a person can gather an instant angry

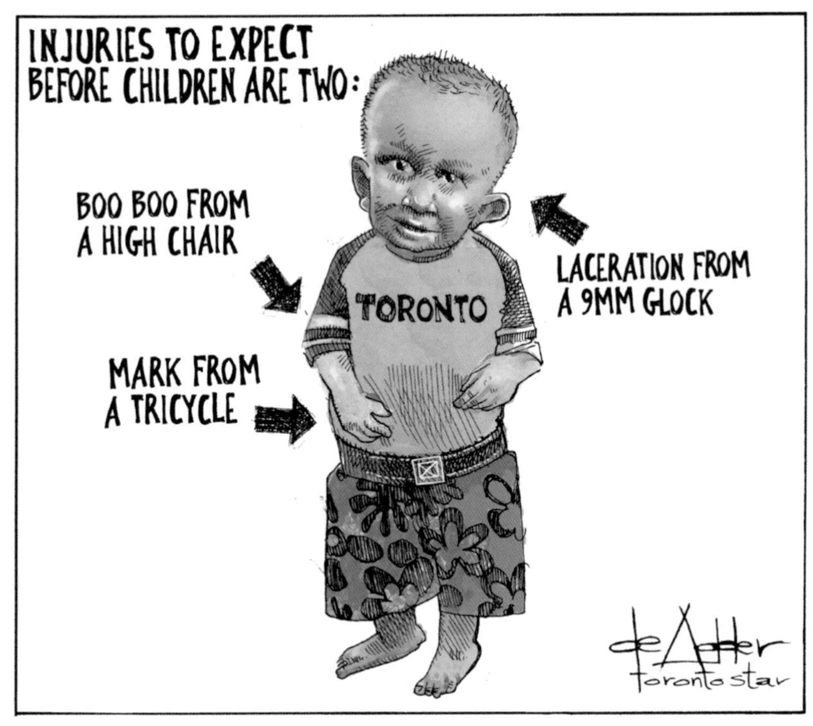


*July 18, 2012. Earlier version of a controversial cartoon that appeared in the* Toronto Star.

*The final version of the cartoon.*

mob without leaving their desk. Before social media and the internet a deluge of letters to the editor was five or six letters. A deluge on social media can be thousands of people. In this age of dwindling newspaper readership, newspapers are more proactive.

On July 17, 2012, there was a shooting in Scarborough at a crowded outdoor party that killed two young people and injured at least nineteen others, including an infant. As a cartoonist, I want to tackle the tough issues as well, so I drew the cartoon above, at left.

I sent this preliminary cartoon to the *Toronto Star*. They asked me to change the gender of the toddler, as well as to take out the 9mm Glock because the type of weapon hadn't been reported.

But then I made a big mistake. I changed "children" to "they." It looked better visually, and the idea was based on the popular "What to Expect" book series, so it sounded better.

Then something completely unforeseen happened.

Many people took issue with my use of the word "they." Readers felt "they" was derogatory towards black people, and believed I was purposely trying to paint a difference between black toddlers and white toddlers. When it was pointed out to me, I saw the point of their argument. I tried to explain that it was an editing error and by "they" I meant "children," but it was too late.

Twitter went off the rails again. I was attacked on Facebook. It became a national story. I went on CBC's *The Current* to explain myself and got raked over the coals by their panellists. It was very difficult because the people who took issue with the way the cartoon was portrayed had a point. It could be interpreted in two ways.

The *Toronto Star* decided to apologize for the error, and I supported that decision on the basis that the cartoon had an unintended second interpretation.

Then there are times when a paper refuses to apologize.

When it was reported that seventy-three Nova Scotia government union jobs would be outsourced, I drew Nova Scotia Government & General Employees Union president Joan Jessome leaving premier Darrel Dexter's bed, with Dexter saying "I'll call you." Jessome didn't like the cartoon.

*November 8, 2012. Dozens of government information technology workers are bracing for news Thursday morning that their jobs will be contracted out to IBM Canada. It seemed the love was lost between Joan Jessome and Darrell Dexter.*

Her reaction surprised me. I thought Jessome had a thicker skin and a better sense of humour. She wrote a letter to the editor of the *Chronicle-Herald*, saying the cartoon was humiliating, sexist, and offensive, and that I'd never do the same thing if she was a man. To prove she was wrong, the next week I drew a similar cartoon, only this time it was Darrell Dexter in bed with a man.

The *Chronicle-Herald* gives the cartoonist the freedom to make their point. Not all newspapers are like this.

In 2007 I came out with my first collection of editorial cartoons. I didn't know it at the time, but that would be my last book of editorial cartoons while working for the *Daily News*. The newspaper folded four months later.

This new book in your hands is work I have done since that time.

When you freelance you're basically a gun for hire, so the cartoons in this collection have been published in various publications. Most appeared in the *Chronicle-Herald*, but also included are cartoons I've done for the *Moncton Times & Transcript*, *Fredericton Daily Gleaner*, *Toronto Star*, *Hill Times*, *Embassy*, and *Canadian Business Journal*. What can I say? I'm a busy cartoonist. I'm not sure how I found time for a book.

*February 8, 2009. Stephen Harper and Mike Duffy.*

# Nova Scotia

*December 4, 2011.*

*November 12, 2012. Halifax's famous height restrictions.*

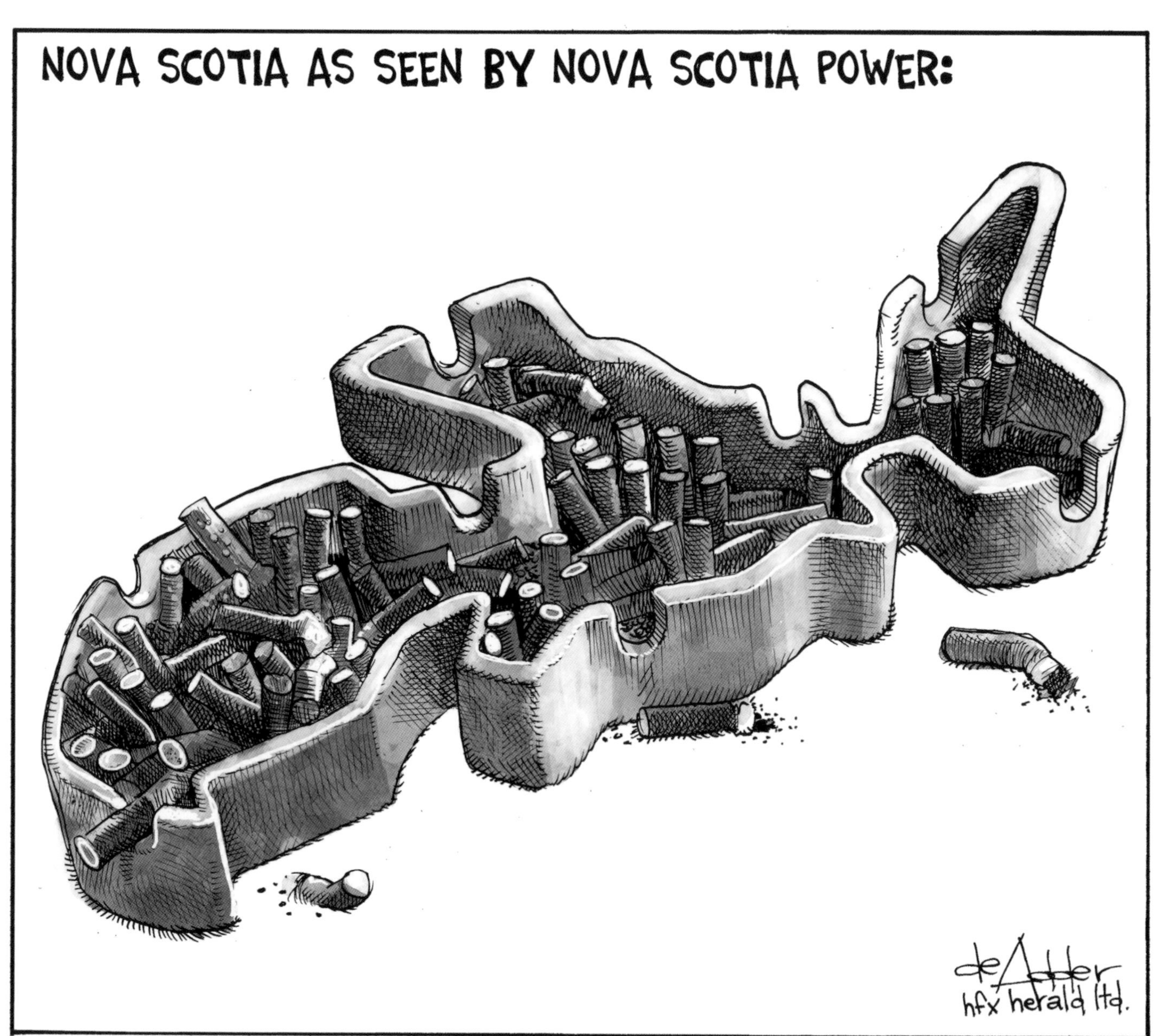
NOVA SCOTIA AS SEEN BY NOVA SCOTIA POWER:
deAdder
hfx herald ltd.

June 8, 2013.

August 2, 2012.

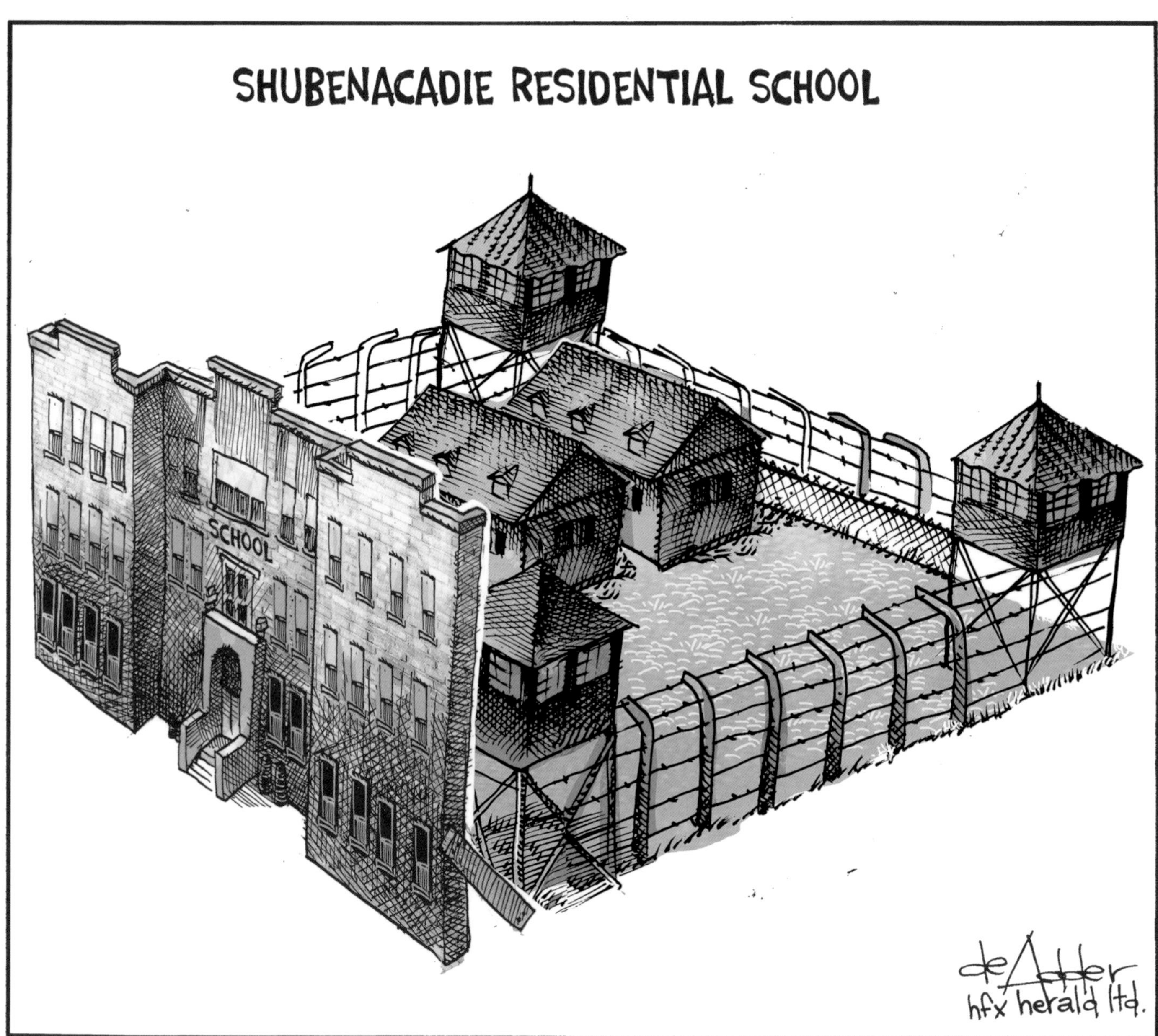
SHUBENACADIE RESIDENTIAL SCHOOL
SCHOOL
de Adder
hfx herald ltd.

*July 19, 2013.*

*October 19, 2012. Halifax elects a new mayor, Mike Savage, to replace Peter Kelly.*

September 8, 2012.

*October 16, 2012. Justin Trudeau visits Nova Scotia, which gave provincial Liberal leader Stephen McNeil the chance to boost his fortunes.*

THE TENTATIVE DEAL WITH PARAMEDICS CAME JUST IN TIME.
EHS
EHS
POLL
de Adder
hfx herald ltd.

June 13, 2013.

*September 11, 2012. Heavy rains caused localized flooding in parts of Nova Scotia, especially Truro.*

*February 19, 2013. A month before Rehtaeh Parsons took her own life, the provincial government seemed to be burying the report on bullying.*

*February 20, 2013. Mayor Mike Savage and the city want a new deal over bottle collection.*

*March 8, 2013. The province tries to do something about cellphone contracts.*

*March 8, 2013. The NDP government seems intent on delaying an election for as long as possible.*

*March 15, 2013. A woman who worked for former Liberal cabinet minister Russell Mackinnon says he offered her a bonus if she agreed to buy his car.*

March 25, 2013.

*April 11, 2013. Rehtaeh Parsons's death draws calls for the RCMP to reopen her case.*

# New Brunswick

*January 31, 2010. It is announced that U2 will play on Magnetic Hill.*

*April 9, 2009. ACDC announces they will play Magnetic Hill in August.*

*April 17, 2009. The Frye Festival in Moncton coincides with details of ACDC playing Magnetic Hill.*

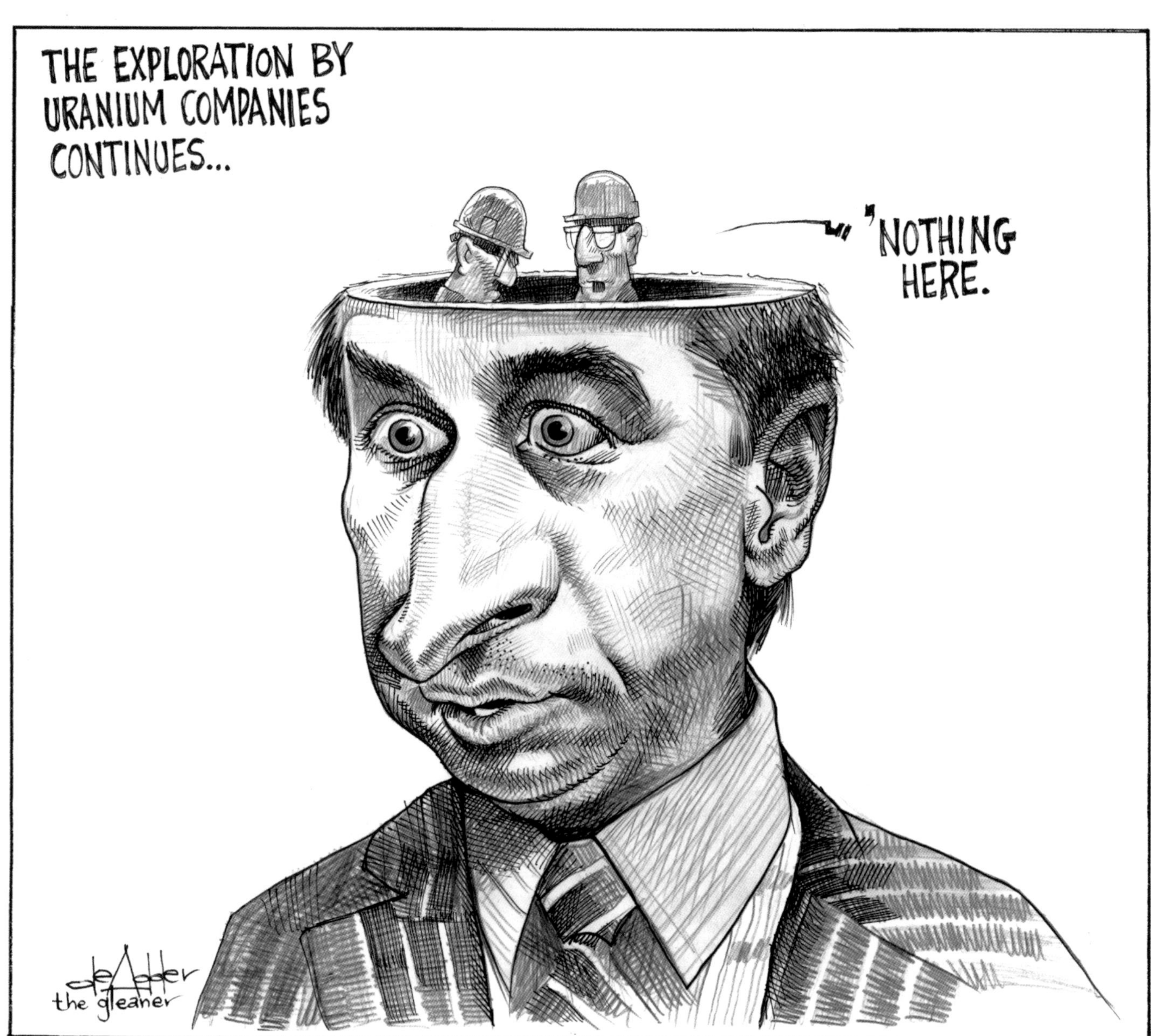


*June 5, 2008. The issue of uranium mining was on the front burner. Shawn Graham didn't seem to have a clear position.*

*November 10, 2010. Shawn Graham steps down as leader of the Liberals.*

*April 23, 2011. Calls to privatize New Brunswick Liquor Corporation go nowhere.*

*December 2, 2010. Bernard Lord says "sacred cows" might have to be sacrificed due to the province's debt.*

*November 24, 2012.*

January 10, 2013.

*July 17, 2013. Alex Colville dies.*

*February 22, 2013. Shawn Graham quits politics after a conflict of interest scandal.*

*February 25, 2013. When it was announced there would be a byelection in the riding of Kent, newly minted Liberal leader Brian Gallant balked before deciding to run.*

*March 15, 2013. The RCMP plans to close between twelve and fifteen satellite offices around New Brunswick.*

*April 4, 2013. Efficiency NB cuts six jobs and suspends programs. Meanwhile, government patronage appointee and CEO Margaret-Ann Blaney is on vacation.*

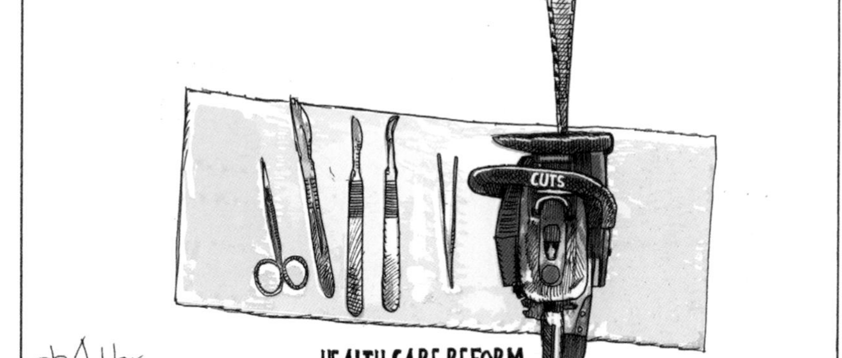


*April 19, 2013. Health care reform in New Brunswick comes with an unprecedented number of cuts.*

*November 12, 2010. Mount Allsion is voted the number one undergraduate university for the umpteeth time.*

# Toronto

*November 28, 2010.*
*Rob Ford takes power in Toronto.*

*November 27, 2011.*

*November 29, 2011. Mayor Rob Ford looks to axe nutrition program.*

*July 27, 2011. Councillor Doug Ford fires back at library cuts critics, including Margaret Atwood. Ford says, "I've got more libraries in my area than I have Tim Hortons."*

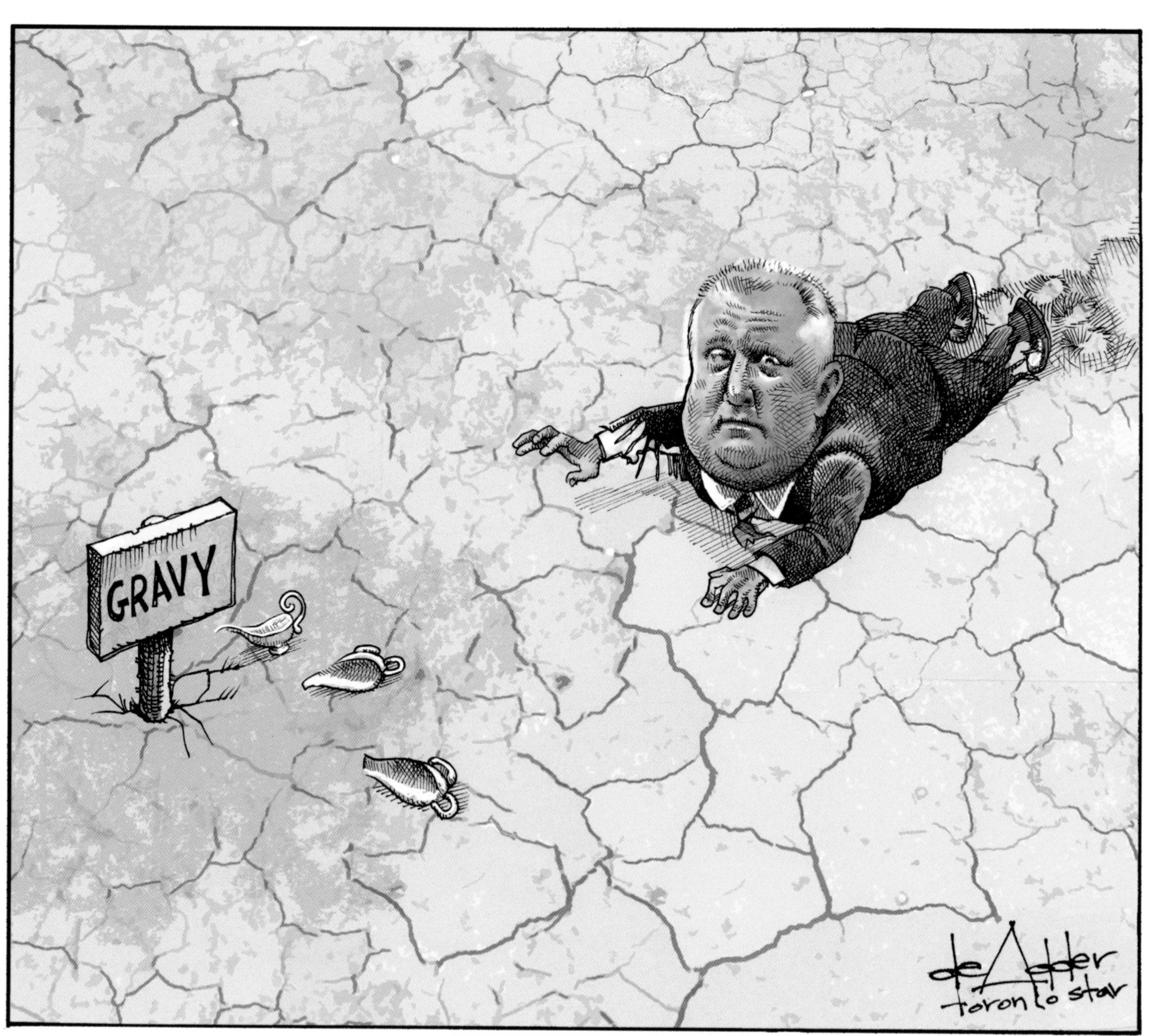


*July 19, 2011. Rob Ford vows to end the "gravy train."*

*May 18, 2013. Toronto Mayor Rob Ford and Senator Mike Duffy.*

BUS
DON MILLS
STREETCAR
QUEEN
SUBWAY
SHEPPARD
ROLLERCOASTER
SCARBOROUGH
deAdder
torontostar

*July 17, 2013.*

*May 31, 2011. The Winnipeg Jets return to the NHL.*

May 4, 2013.

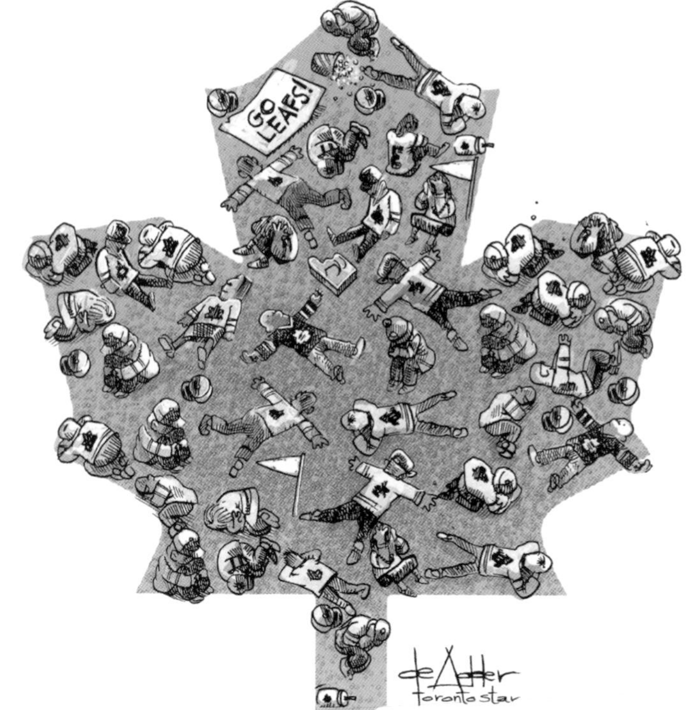


May 15, 2013. The Toronto Maple Leafs lose game seven to the Boston Bruins.

*September 9, 2011. Toronto International Film Festival (TIFF).*

*September 4, 2012. TIFF has changed over the years, from arthouse to Hollywood.*

*September 11, 2012. Members of a world-renowned string quartet struggle to stay together in the face of death, competing egos and insuppressible lust. Mark Ivanir, Christopher Walken, Philip Seymour Hoffman, Catherine Keener.*

*September 7, 2012. Ben Affleck, Victor Garber in Argo.*

*September 12, 2012. TIFF attendees.*

*March 6, 2013. Country legend Stompin' Tom Connors dies.*

# Canada

December 11, 2008.

*September 5, 2008.*

*September 19, 2008. The beginning of the 2008 federal election.*

*November 30, 2008. During the prorogation scandal, Stephen Harper and Jim Flaherty are faced with losing power to a coalition.*

*December 3, 2008. The prorogation scandal heats up while governor general Michaëlle Jean was away.*

*January 8, 2010. Stephen Harper prorogues Parliament for the second time.*

*May 15, 2009. Stephen Harper goes on the attack to define Michael Ignatieff.*

*September 9, 2009. Talk of an election seems to be getting Michael Ignatieff nowhere.*

*April 4, 2010.*

November 27, 2009

August 29, 2009

April 21, 2010.

October 30, 2008.

April 3, 2010.

*April 27, 2010. Federal cabinet minister Bev Oda.*

*September 23, 2011.*

*November 4, 2010. John Baird returns to the environment portfolio.*

*November 12, 2010.*

May 23, 2009.

October 29, 2008. Paul Martin publishes a new book.

*May 15, 2011. Stephen Harper appoints conservatives who lost the last election to the senate.*

March 29, 2011.

*March 3, 2011.
Stephen Harper and
the Conservatives are
accused of election fraud.*

December 19, 2010.

*April 12, 2011. Auditor general Sheila Fraser seems to be the one person Canadians trust.*

*April 13, 2011. The Conservatives talk gun control.*

*April 15, 2011. Election debate produces spin.*

*April 6, 2011. Michael Ignatieff has problems fielding candidates with questionable pasts.*

*April 21, 2011. Stephen Harper starts to sound like a broken record during the 2011 election.*

MR. HARPER, HOW LONG HAVE YOU HAD AN OVERWHELMING NEED TO CONTROL AND MANIPULATE EVERYTHING?
de Adder the gleaner

*April 8, 2011.*

April 26, 2011.

*May 3, 2011. The Conservatives win a majority in the federal election.*

*November 14, 2011. Don Cherry is back in the news for being himself.*

*March 1, 2012. Stephen Harper accused of promoting a culture of deception.*

*September 29, 2011 Stephen Harper's crime agenda includes new prisons.*

*November 22, 2012.*

November 29, 2012.

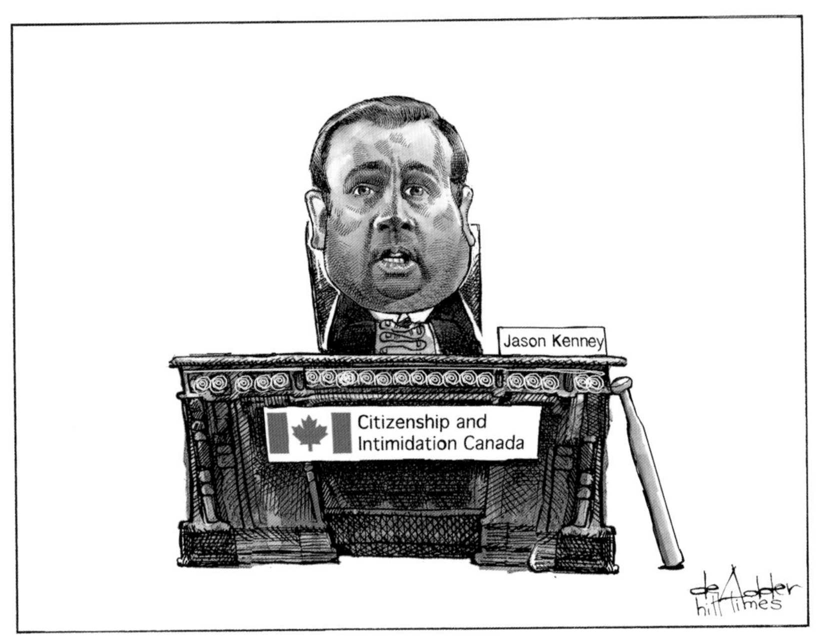


August 3, 2012.

August 28 2012.

*August 23, 2011. Jack Layton passes away.*

*December 22, 2011.*

*February 21, 2010. John Babcock, the last living Canadian soldier from the First World War, dies.*

*October 28, 2011. An often-misunderstood cartoon. Occupy people thought I was undermining their movement; however my intention was to show the veteran comparing his exploits when he was young to the exploits of the Occupy movement.*

*May 6, 2010. Anniversary of the liberation of Holland.*

*November 12, 2012.*

*July 13, 2009. Tim Hortons opens in New York.*

*February 6, 2010. The CRTC rules on modern internet usage.*

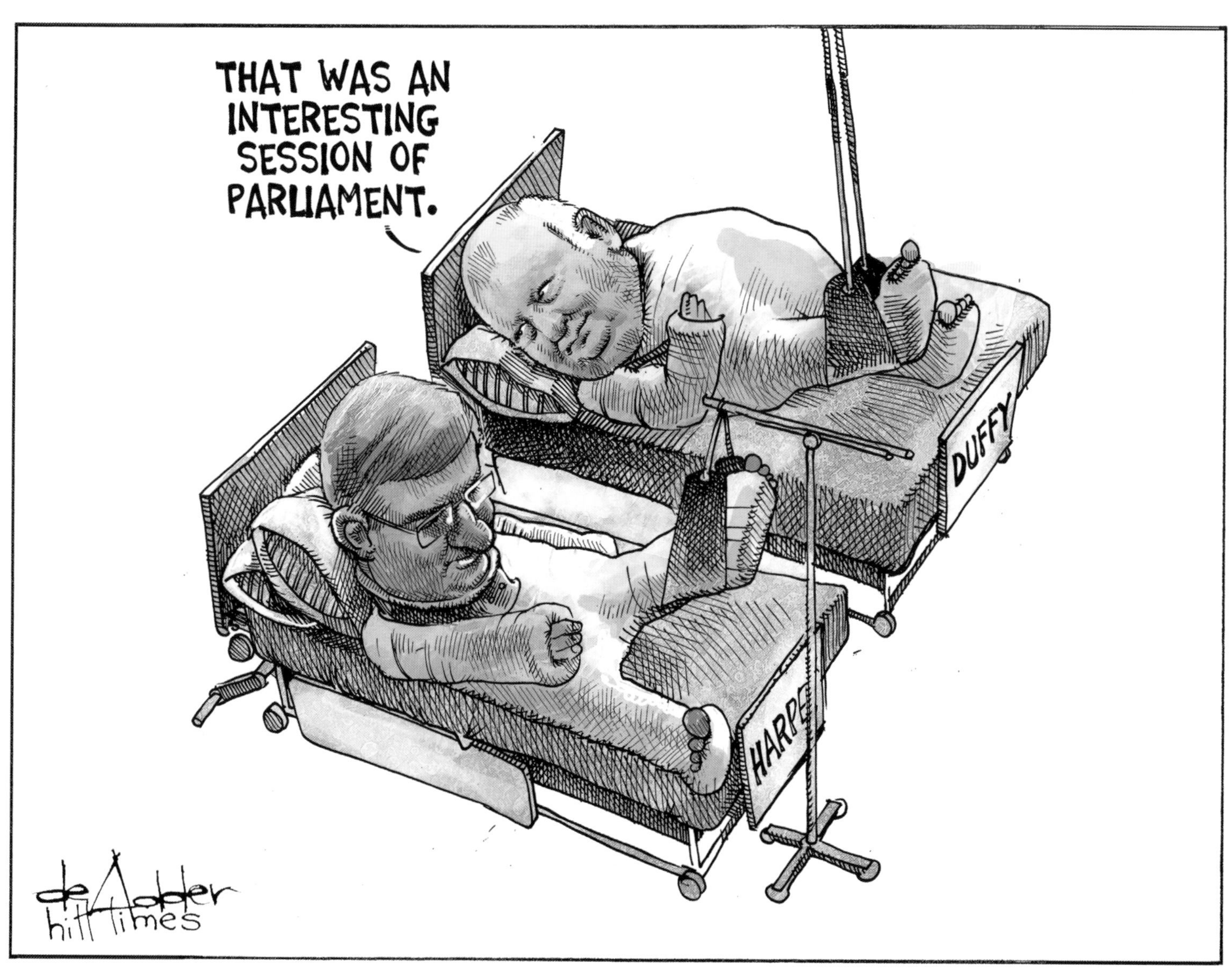
THAT WAS AN INTERESTING SESSION OF PARLIAMENT.
DUFFY
HARPE
deAdder
hill times

June 24, 2013.

*May 30, 2011. Will and Kate's visit to Canada includes the Calgary Stampede.*

*October 15, 2012. Amanda Todd, a bullied teen, shares her story and then commits suicide.*

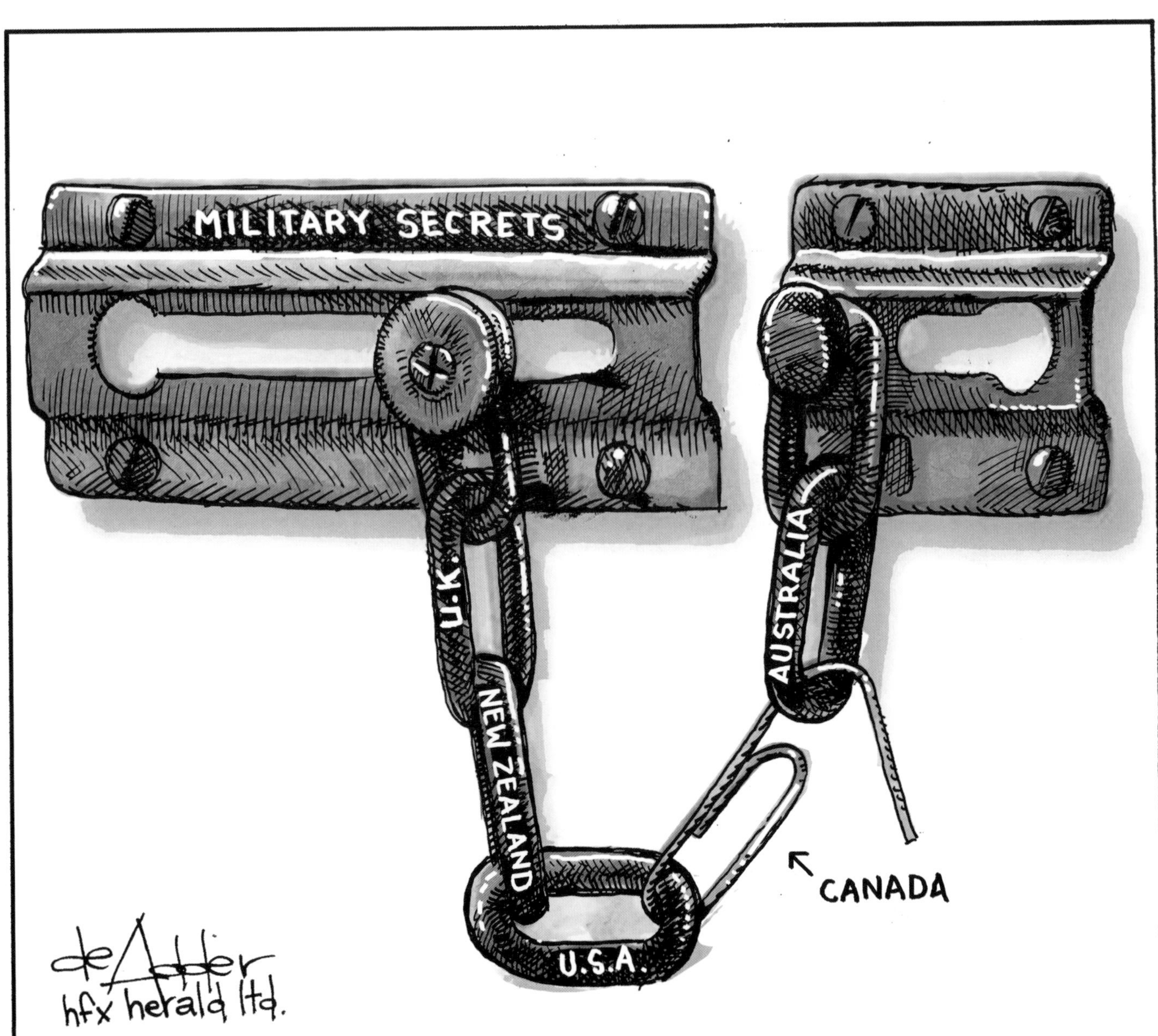


*February 1, 2013. A Halifax spy is convicted.*

*February 15, 2013.*

*February 26, 2013. Getting tough on EI claimants instead of Senators.*

April 19, 2013.

February 21, 2013.

*March 28, 2013. Stephen Harper puts down a small revolt in his caucus.*

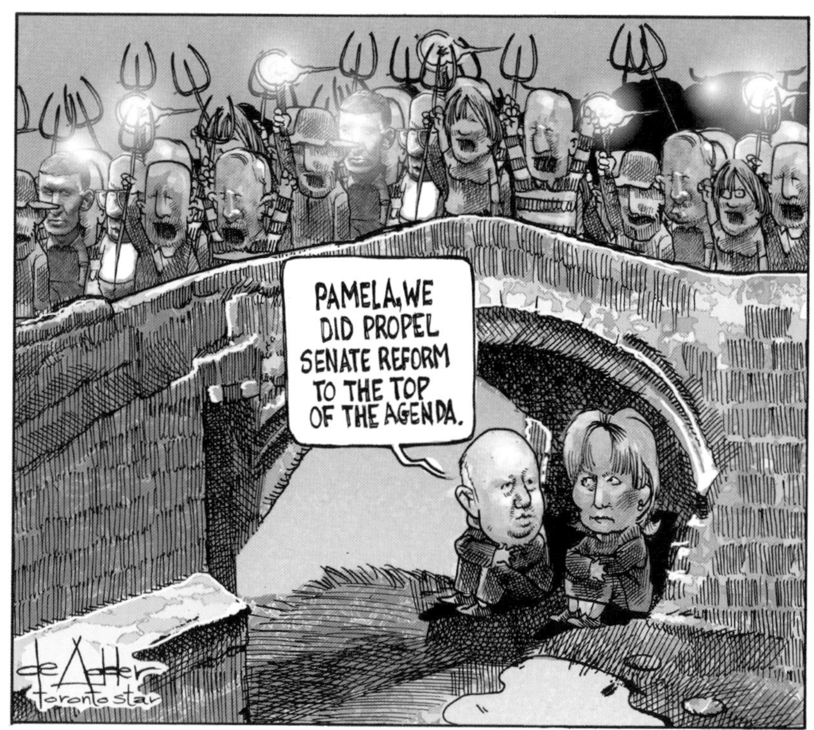


*February 26, 2013. Pamela Wallin and Mike Duffy.*

April 11, 2013. Justin Trudeau wins the Liberal leadership.

April 18, 2013.

THAT REALLY IS JUSTIN TRUDEAU.

THIS LEADERSHIP RACE HAS DRAGGED ON FOR SO LONG THAT HE JUST LOOKS LIKE THAT NOW.

JUSTIN

deAdder
hfx herald ltd.

April 5, 2013.

# World

*September 26, 2008. Sarah Palin and John McCain.*

January 20, 2009.

April 23, 2009.

November 5, 2008.

March 24, 2009.

*September 22, 2009.*

*October 28, 2011. Recession hits the United States.*

November 25, 2010.

*December 24, 2010. "Don't touch my junk," one of the catchphrases of the times.*

*August 5, 2011. Economic woes continue.*

*September 9, 2011. Ten years since 9-11.*

*February 11, 2013. Pope Benedict retires.*

*March 29, 2010. The Pope demonstrates that he is not a modernizer.*

*March 23, 2011. The tsunami in Japan occurs as the war in Libya heats up.*

*April 26, 2009. Swine flu panic.*

*January 6, 2011.*

*September 1, 2012.*

March 7, 2011. Libya's Muammar Gaddafi.

October 20, 2009. Afghanistan election.

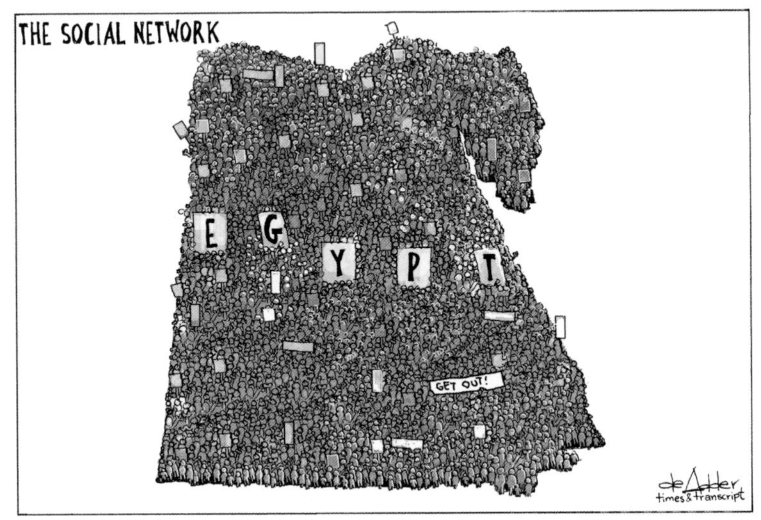


February 4, 2010. The Arab Spring includes Egypt.

September 21, 2009.

*May 1, 2013. The collapse of a Bangladesh clothing factory kills over 1,000 people.*

*December 18, 2012. Four days after the Newtown shootings.*

*April 8, 2013. Margaret Thatcher and Reveen the Impossibilist die.*

*April 4, 2013. John Baird and Benjamin Netanyahu.*

December 12, 2012.